GW00702933

Illustrations copyright
© 1999 Jacqueline Mair
This edition copyright
© 1999 Lion Publishing

Published by
Lion Publishing plc
Sandy Lane West,
Oxford, England
www.lion-publishing.co.uk
ISBN 0 7459 3998 8

First edition 1999
10 9 8 7 6 5 4 3 2 1 0

A catalogue record for
this book is available
from the British Library

Typeset in Venetian 301
Printed and bound
in Singapore

Acknowledgments

We would like to thank all
those who have given us
permission to include material
in this book. Every effort has
been made to trace and
acknowledge copyright holders
of all the quotations included.
We apologize for any errors or
omissions that may remain,
and would ask those
concerned to contact the
publishers, who will ensure
that full acknowledgment is
made in the future.

pp. 14, 19, 23, 36, 44, 51, 56:
Scripture quotations taken
from the *Good News Bible*
published by The Bible
Societies/HarperCollins
Publishers Ltd, UK ©
American Bible Society, 1966,
1971, and 4th edition 1976.

♥ H E A R T F E L T S

In My Thoughts

COMPILED BY FRANCES GRANT

LION
Giftlines

IN MY THOUGHTS

Many people spend
part of their lives in a
      separate place
      from the ones
      they love.
      The writings
    contained here
    paint a fond
picture of heartfelt
good wishes, of those

who are thinking of
others and longing to
keep in touch. This in
itself is comforting,
yet it also reveals a
greater truth — that
God is thinking about
us, not just now, but
always; and in that we
are all united, wherever
we may be.

We haven't been doing much since you guys left. Life is boring without you. Well, a lot less exciting, because bored people are boring people. Yep, it was definitely more exciting when you were around. *WE MISS YOU!!!!!!!!!!!!!!!*

ADASSA (AGED ELEVEN)

How ardently
I long for
your return.

ABIGAIL ADAMS

♥

Whatever you can do,
or dream you can,
begin it;
boldness has genius,
power and magic in it;
begin it now.

JOHANN WOLFGANG VON GOETHE

♥

And I will be with you always, to the end of the age.

FROM THE NEW TESTAMENT
GOSPEL OF MATTHEW

♥

I looked out my window
at the waves on the lake,
the vivid blue sky, and
even the flotsam in the
cove next to my place,
and thought about how
similar lives can be,
even at great distances.

BOB BROWN

Dear Dad,
Hope the rig's OK and
the sea's not too rough.
Mairi's tooth's come out
and Jimmy's teacher says
his sums are worse, and
me and Mum think the
rabbit's missing you.
But don't worry.
Just come home now.

JENNY (AGED NINE)

Peace
be with you.

FROM THE NEW TESTAMENT
GOSPEL OF LUKE

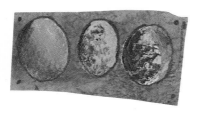

Ah! When will
this long weary
day have end,
and lend me
leave to come
unto my love?

EDMUND SPENSER

It was the
time of roses,
We plucked them
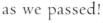
as we passed!

THOMAS HOOD

Don't ask me
to leave you!
Let me go with you.
Wherever you go,
I will go; wherever
you live,
I will live.

FROM THE OLD TESTAMENT
BOOK OF RUTH

I do love
nothing in the
world *so well
as you*: is not
that strange?

WILLIAM SHAKESPEARE

How are the exams going, honey? I hope that you're not stressing too much. You must have Physics on Tuesday, so good luck. Only six more to go.

ALISON SIMPSON

I'm so excited that you're finally coming to visit! I got your e-mail after we spoke. Anyway, you now know that there's enough room for you and the boys — we can all squeeze in.

RON SIN-SHU

It is emphatically your business now to look forwards and not backwards: and also to look forwards in an eager and optimistic spirit.

EVELYN UNDERHILL

I do not regret that this
separation has been,
for it is worth no small
sacrifice to be thus
assured that instead of
weakening, our union
has strengthened —
a hundredfold
strengthened.

MARY WORDSWORTH

'Tis distance lends
enchantment
to the view,
and robes the
mountain in its
azure hue.

THOMAS CAMPBELL

The distance
is nothing;
it is only the
first step that
is difficult.

MADAME DU DEFFAND

There is nothing
either good
or bad,
but thinking
makes it so.

WILLIAM SHAKESPEARE

I will see you
again, and
your hearts
will be filled
with gladness.

FROM THE NEW TESTAMENT
GOSPEL OF JOHN

Golden slumbers
kiss your eyes,
smiles awake you
when you rise.

THOMAS DEKKER

Will you,
won't you,
will you,
won't you,
will you join
the dance?

LEWIS CARROLL

More than
kisses, letters
mingle souls.

JOHN DONNE

I prize thy love
more than whole
mines of gold.

ANNE BRADSTREET

Live all
you can;
it's a mistake
not to.

HENRY JAMES

Those who are
good travel a road
that avoids evil;
so watch where
you are going — it
may save your life.

FROM THE OLD TESTAMENT
BOOK OF PROVERBS

And if thou wilt, remember, and if thou wilt, forget.

CHRISTINA ROSSETTI

Many men go
fishing all of
their lives without
knowing that it
is not fish they
are after.

HENRY DAVID THOREAU

If you are at Rome
live in the Roman
style; if you are
elsewhere live as
they live elsewhere.

ST AMBROSE

It was very good
of you to help me
in my troubles…
and so I send
greetings to all
of God's people.

FROM THE NEW TESTAMENT
LETTER TO THE PHILIPPIANS

Some relationships
just seem to work,
despite so many
obstacles and
demands that
we create.

DAVID VACHELL

Know you the
land where…
the gold oranges
glow? A soft wind
hovers from the
sky, the myrtle is
still and the laurel

♥

stands tall. There,
there, I would go,
O my beloved,
with thee!

JOHANN WOLFGANG VON GOETHE

There are many rooms
in my Father's house,
and I am going to
prepare a place for you.
I would not tell you this
if it were not so.

FROM THE NEW TESTAMENT
GOSPEL OF JOHN

♥

I'm back home again and I have cooked dinner, done the laundry, and watered one of a million plants. I can't believe how tiring it is — I guess because I'm missing you. Write back immediately!

CHRIS ANDO

♥

You need not miss me. I am thinking of you, and am only around the corner. I will be here when you come home.

FROM A FATHER'S LETTER
TO HIS SON IN FLANDERS, 1943